62nd Annual Meeting of the Association for Computational Linguistics (ACL 2024)

AA004793

Tutorial Abstracts

Bangkok, Thailand
11-16 August 2024

ISBN: 979-8-3313-0152-1

Printed from e-media with permission by:

Curran Associates, Inc.
57 Morehouse Lane
Red Hook, NY 12571

proceedings.com

Some format issues inherent in the e-media version may also appear in this print version.

Copyright© (2024) by the Association for Computational Linguistics
All rights reserved.

Printed with permission by Curran Associates, Inc. (2024)

For permission requests, please contact the Association for Computational Linguistics
at the address below.

Association for Computational Linguistics
209 N. Eighth Street
Stroudsburg, Pennsylvania 18360

Phone: 1-570-476-8006
Fax: 1-570-476-0860

acl@aclweb.org

Additional copies of this publication are available from:

Curran Associates, Inc.
57 Morehouse Lane
Red Hook, NY 12571 USA
Phone: 845-758-0400
Fax: 845-758-2633
Email: curran@proceedings.com
Web: www.proceedings.com

ACL 2024

The 62nd Annual Meeting of the Association for Computational Linguistics

Proceedings of the Tutorial Abstracts

August 11-16, 2024

©2024 Association for Computational Linguistics

Order copies of this and other ACL proceedings from:

Association for Computational Linguistics (ACL)
317 Sidney Baker St. S
Suite 400 - 134
Kerrville, TX 78028
USA
Tel: +1-855-225-1962
acl@aclweb.org

Introduction

Welcome to this year's ACL tutorial session, a highlight of our conference. We are thrilled to have you with us!

The ACL tutorial session aims to provide attendees with a thorough introduction to key topics in our fast-evolving research field, delivered by expert researchers. This year, as in recent years, the process of calling for, submitting, reviewing, and selecting tutorials was a collaborative effort across multiple conferences: EACL, NAACL, ACL, and EMNLP.

We assembled a review committee consisting of the tutorial chairs from EACL (Sharid Loaiciga, Mohsen Mesgar), NAACL (Rui Zhang, Nathan Schneider, Snigdha Chaturvedi), and the interim EMNLP tutorial chair (Isabelle Augenstein). Each tutorial proposal was meticulously reviewed by a panel of three reviewers, who assessed them based on criteria such as clarity, preparedness, novelty, timeliness, instructors' experience, potential audience, open access to teaching materials, and diversity (including multilingualism, gender, age, and geolocation). Out of 27 submissions, 6 were selected for presentation at ACL.

We would like to thank the tutorial authors for their commitment, dedicated collaboration and flexibility while organizing the conference. Finally, our thanks go to the conference organizers for effective collaboration, and in particular to the general chair Claire Gardent.

Enjoy the session!

Warm regards,
ACL 2024 Tutorial Co-chairs
Luis Chiruzzo
Hung-yi Lee
Leonardo F. R. Ribeiro

Table of Contents

Program

Sunday, August 11, 2024

09:00 - 12:30	*Tutorial 1 - Computational Linguistics for Brain Encoding and Decoding: Principles, Practices and Beyond*
09:00 - 12:30	*Tutorial 2 - Automatic and Human-AI Interactive Text Generation (with a focus on Text Simplification and Revision)*
09:00 - 12:30	*Tutorial 3 - Vulnerabilities of Large Language Models to Adversarial Attacks*
14:00 - 17:30	*Tutorial 4 - Computational Expressivity of Neural Language Models*
14:00 - 17:30	*Tutorial 5 - Watermarking for Large Language Models*
14:00 - 17:30	*Tutorial 6 - Presentation Matters: How to Communicate Science in the NLP Venues and in the Wild?*

Computational Linguistics for Brain Encoding and Decoding: Principles, Practices and Beyond

Jingyuan Sun **Shaonan Wang** **Zijiao Chen** **Jixing Li** **Marie-Francine Moens**

Computational linguistics (CL) has witnessed tremendous advancements in recent years, with models such as large language models demonstrating exceptional performance in various natural language processing tasks. These advancements highlight their potential to help understand brain language processing, especially through the lens of brain encoding and decoding. Brain encoding involves the mapping of linguistic stimuli to brain activity, while brain decoding is the process of reconstructing linguistic stimuli from observed brain activities. CL models that excel at capturing and manipulating linguistic features are crucial for mapping linguistic stimuli to brain activities and vice versa. Brain encoding and decoding have vast applications, from enhancing human-computer interaction to developing assistive technologies for individuals with communication impairments. This tutorial will focus on elucidating how computational linguistics can facilitate brain encoding and decoding. We will delve into the principles and practices of using computational linguistics methods for brain encoding and decoding. We will also discuss the challenges and future directions of brain encoding and decoding. Through this tutorial, we aim to provide a comprehensive and informative overview of the intersection between computational linguistics and cognitive neuroscience, inspiring future research in this exciting and rapidly evolving field.

Jingyuan Sun, Postdoc researcher in the Department of Computer Science, KU Leuven, Belgium
email: `jingyuan.sun@kuleuven.be`
website: `https://www.kuleuven.be/wieiswie/en/person/00155742`
Jingyuan Sun has published papers in artificial intelligence and natural language processing journals and conferences such as TNNLS, Scientific Data, AAAI, IJCAI, EMNLP, COLING, ECAI, etc. He also serves as a (senior) PC member for these above conferences. He is a reviewer of TPAMI.

Shaonan Wang, Associate Professor in the State Key Laboratory of Multimodal Artificial Intelligence System, Institute of Automation, Chinese Academy of Sciences
email: `shaonan.wang@nlpr.ia.ac.cn`
website: `https://wangshaonan.github.io/`
Shaonan Wang has contributed papers to natural language processing journals and conferences such as Information Sciences, TNNLS, ACL, EMNLP, AAAI, and IJCAI. Her work also spans neurolinguistics, with publications in Scientific Data, Brain and language, Cognitive, Affective, and Behavioral Neuroscience, and more. She serves as an editor for Neurobiology of Language and TALLIP and holds the role of curriculum chair at Neuromatch Academy.

Jixing Li, Assistant Professor at in the Department of Linguistics and Translation at the City University of Hong Kong
email: `jixingli@cityu.edu.hk`
website: `https://jixing-li.github.io/`
Jixing Li is an Assistant Professor at in the Department of Linguistics and Translation at the City University of Hong Kong. Her research combines NLP models and neuroimaging methods to examine syntactic and semantic analyses in the brain. Her work has been published in the Journal of Neuroscience, Brain and Language, Annual Review of Linguistics, etc. She serves as an ad-hoc reviewer for top journals in the field of neurolinguistics and is on the editorial board of Communications Psychology.

Zijiao Chen, PhD candidate in the Multimodal Neuroimaging in Neuropsychiatric Disorders Laboratory at the National University of Singapore
email: `zijiao.chen@u.nus.edu`
Zijiao Chen is a PhD candidate in the Multimodal

Proceedings of the 62nd Annual Meeting of the Association for Computational Linguistics (Volume 5: Tutorial Abstracts), pages 1–2
August 11-16, 2024 ©2024 Association for Computational Linguistics

Neuroimaging in Neuropsychiatric Disorders Laboratory at the National University of Singapore. Her research primarily centers on representation learning within neuroimaging data and brain decoding. She has published papers in artificial intelligence and neuroimage conferences and journals such as CVPR, OHBM, NCAA, and AD.

Marie-Francine Moens, Full Professor in the Department of Computer Science, KU Leuven
email: `sien.moens@cs.kuleuven.be`
website: `https://people.cs.kuleuven.be/~sien.moens/`
Marie-Francine Moens is a Full Professor in the Department of Computer Science, KU Leuven. She is a fellow of the European Laboratory for Learning and Intelligent Systems (ELLIS). She is an associate editor of the journal IEEE Transactions on Pattern Analysis and Machine Intelligence (TPAMI). She holds the ERC Advanced Grant CALCULUS (2018-2024) granted by the European Research Council. She used to be the chair of the European Chapter of the Association for Computational Linguistics (EACL) and was a member of the executive board of the Association for Computational Linguistics (ACL). From 2012 to 2016 she was the coordinator of the MUSE project financed by Future and Emerging Technologies (FET) - Open of the European Commission.

Automatic and Human-AI Interactive Text Generation
(with a focus on Text Simplification and Revision)

Yao Dou **Philippe Laban** **Claire Gardent** **Wei Xu**

In this tutorial, we focus on text-to-text generation, a class of natural language generation (NLG) tasks, that takes a piece of text as input and then generates a revision that is improved according to some specific criteria (e.g., readability or linguistic styles), while largely retaining the original meaning and the length of the text. This includes many useful applications, such as text simplification, paraphrase generation, style transfer, etc. In contrast to text summarization and open-ended text completion (e.g., story), the text-to-text generation tasks we discuss in this tutorial are more constrained in terms of semantic consistency and targeted language styles. This level of control makes these tasks ideal testbeds for studying the ability of models to generate text that is both semantically adequate and stylistically appropriate. Moreover, these tasks are interesting from a technical standpoint, as they require complex combinations of lexical and syntactical transformations, stylistic control, and adherence to factual knowledge, – all at once. With a special focus on text simplification and revision, this tutorial aims to provide an overview of the state-of-the-art natural language generation research from four major aspects – Data, Models, Human-AI Collaboration, and Evaluation – and to discuss and showcase a few significant and recent advances: (1) the use of non-retrogressive approaches; (2) the shift from fine-tuning to prompting with large language models; (3) the development of new learnable metric and fine-grained human evaluation framework; (4) a growing body of studies and datasets on non-English languages; (5) the rise of HCI+NLP+Accessibility interdisciplinary research to create real-world writing assistant systems.

Yao Dou, Ph.D. student in the College of Computing at the Georgia Institute of Technology
email: `douy@gatech.edu`
website: `https://yao-dou.github.io/`
Yao Dou is a Ph.D. student in the College of Computing at the Georgia Institute of Technology, advaised by Prof. Wei Xu. His research interests lie in natural language processing and machine learning. His recent work focuses on text simplification, text evaluation, and social media privacy.

Philippe Laban, Research Scientist at Salesforce Research
email: `plaban@salesforce.com`
website: `https://tingofurro.github.io/`
Philippe Laban is a Research Scientist at Salesforce Research. His research is at the intersection of NLP and HCI, focusing on several tasks within text generation, including text simplification and summarization. He received his Ph.D. in Computer Science from UC Berkeley in 2021. His thesis is titled "Unsupervised Text Generation and its Application to News Interfaces". His recent work has focused on expanding the scope of text simplification to the paragraph and document-level and evaluating textediting interfaces. He publishes in both *ACL and HCI conferences, including work on interactive user interface design for NLP applications.

Claire Gardent, Senior Research Scientist at the French National Center for Scientific Research (CNRS)
email: `claire.gardent@loria.fr`
website: `https://members.loria.fr/CGardent/`
Claire Gardent is a Senior Research Scientist at the French National Center for Scientific Research (CNRS), based at the LORIA Computer Science research unit in Nancy, France. In 2022, she was selected as an ACL Fellow and was awarded the CNRS Silver Medal. She works in the field of NLP with a particular interest in Natural Language Generation. In 2017, she launched the WebNLG challenge, a shared task where the goal is to generate text from Knowledge Base fragments. She

Proceedings of the 62nd Annual Meeting of the Association for Computational Linguistics (Volume 5: Tutorial Abstracts), pages 3–4
August 11-16, 2024 ©2024 Association for Computational Linguistics

has proposed neural models for simplification and summarization; for the generation of long-form documents such as multi-document summaries and Wikipedia articles; for multilingual generation from Abstract Meaning Representations and for response generation in dialog. She currently heads the AI XNLG Chair on multi-lingual, multi-source NLG and the CNRS LIFT Research Network on Computational, Formal and Field Linguistics

Wei Xu, Assistant Professor in the College of Computing at the Georgia Institute of Technology
email: `wei.xu@cc.gatech.edu`
website: `https://cocoxu.github.io/`
Wei Xu is an Assistant Professor in the College of Computing at the Georgia Institute of Technology. Her recent research focuses on text generation (including data construction, controllable model, human and automatic evaluation), stylistics, analyzing and evaluating large language models (including multilingual capability, cross-lingual transfer learning, cultural bias, and cost efficiency). She is a recipient of the NSF CAREER Award, CrowdFlower AI for Everyone Award, best paper award from COLING 2018, and honorable mention from ACL 2023. She is an NAACL executive board member and regularly serves as a (senior) area chair for *ACL conferences. She frequently gives invited talks at universities and companies. She has given tutorials on "NLP for Social Media and Text Analysis" and has organized multiple workshops, including WNUT, GEM, and TSAR.

Computational Expressivity of Neural Language Models

Alexandra Butoi **Ryan Cotterell** **Anej Svete**

Language models (LMs) are currently at the forefront of NLP research due to their remarkable versatility across diverse tasks. However, a large gap exists between their observed capabilities and the explanations proposed by established formal machinery. To motivate a better theoretical characterization of LMs' abilities and limitations, this tutorial aims to provide a comprehensive introduction to a specific framework for formal analysis of modern LMs using tools from formal language theory (FLT). We present how tools from FLT can be useful in understanding the inner workings and predicting the capabilities of modern neural LM architectures. We will cover recent results using FLT to make precise and practically relevant statements about LMs based on recurrent neural networks and transformers by relating them to formal devices such as finite-state automata, Turing machines, and analog circuits. Altogether, the results covered in this tutorial will allow us to make precise statements and explanations about the observed as well as predicted behaviors of LMs, as well as provide theoretically motivated suggestions on the aspects of the architectures that could be improved.

Alexandra Butoi, Ph.D. Candidate at ETH Zürich.
email: `alexandra.butoi@inf.ethz.ch`
website: `https://rycolab.io/authors/alexandra/`
Her current interests include formalisms for mildly context-sensitive languages and parsing.

Ryan Cotterell, Assistant professor at ETH Zürich in the Institute for Machine Learning.
email: `ryan.cotterell@inf.ethz.ch`
website: `https://rycolab.io/authors/ryan/`
His research focuses on a wide range of topics, including information-theoretic linguistics, parsing, computational typology and morphology, and bias and fairness in NLP systems.

Anej Svete, Ph.D. Candidate at ETH AI Centre at ETH Zürich.
email: `anej.svete@inf.ethz.ch`
website: `https://anejsvete.github.io/`
His main research interests lie at the intersection of formal language theory and LMs, where he is working on improving our understanding of the formal properties of modern architectures.

Proceedings of the 62nd Annual Meeting of the Association for Computational Linguistics (Volume 5: Tutorial Abstracts), pages 5–5
August 11-16, 2024 ©2024 Association for Computational Linguistics

Presentation Matters: How to Communicate Science in the NLP Venues and in the Wild?

Sarvnaz Karimi, Cecile Paris and Gholamreza Haffari

Each year a large number of early career researchers join the NLP/Computational Linguistics community, with most starting by presenting their research in the *ACL conferences and workshops. While writing a paper that has made it to these venues is one important step, what comes with communicating the outcome is equally important and sets the path to impact of a research outcome. In addition, not all PhD candidates get the chance of being trained for their presentation skills. Research methods courses are not all of the same quality and may not cover scientific communications, and certainly not all are tailored to the NLP community. We are proposing an introductory tutorial that covers a range of different communication skills, including writing, oral presentation (posters and demos), and social media presence. This is to fill in the gap for the researchers who may not have access to research methods courses or other mentors who could help them acquire such skills. The interactive nature of such a tutorial would allow attendees to ask questions and clarifications which would not be possible from reading materials alone.

Sarvnaz Karimi, ACL's Publicity Director (2023-2026), Principal Research Scientist at CSIRO (Australia's National Science Agency).
email: `Sarvnaz.Karimi@csiro.au`
website: `https://people.csiro.au/K/S/Sarvnaz-Karimi`
Dr Sarvnaz Karimi has been an active researcher in NLP and IR for over a decade. She was the president of the Australiasian Language Technology Association (ALTA), where she established a mentoring programme for the Australia-New Zealand NLP researchers seeking mentorship. She is currently acting team leader of the language technology team at CSIRO's Data61. As part of her ACL's publicity responsibilities, she looks after the ACL's social media presence and coordination of the publicity chairs across different conferences, including ACL, NAACL, EACL, AACL and EMNLP. She is currently seeking a tutorial at the ACL conference, as one of the opportunities to engage with the audience to better leverage their social media presence to communicate their research outcomes. Sarvnaz co-presented a tutorial at AACL-IJCNLP 2020 (NLP for Healthcare in the Absence of a Healthcare Dataset). She also actively participates in recruitment interviews for PhD and postdoctoral fellows, which provides her with insight into how writing CVs and interviewing skills can be tailored for jobs in industrial research settings.

Cecile Paris, Chief Research Scientist at Data61, the Director of the Collaborative Intelligence (CINTEL) FSP.

Proceedings of the 62nd Annual Meeting of the Association for Computational Linguistics (Volume 5: Tutorial Abstracts), pages 6–7
August 11-16, 2024 ©2024 Association for Computational Linguistics

email: Cecile.Paris@csiro.au
website: https://people.csiro.au/p/c/cecile-paris
Dr Cecile Paris the Director of CINTEL FSP, a CSIRO-wide research programme about leveraging the intelligence and capabilities of humans and machines to form the best-performing teams. She received her PhD in Artificial Intelligence (AI) (more specifically in Natural Language Processing and User Modelling) in 1987 from Columbia University (New York). Her research has focused on Natural Language Processing and User Modelling throughout her career. She joined the Information Sciences Institute (ISI), an AI research laboratory in Marina del Rey (Los Angeles, CA), where she stayed until 1996, working on knowledge-based systems and Explainable AI. She then moved to the UK (ITRI, at the University of Brighton, UK), where she researched multilingual generation systems. She joined CSIRO in late 1996, creating the Natural Language Processing team. She was elected a Fellow of the Australian Academy of Technology & Engineering (ATSE) in 2016 and a Fellow of the Royal Society of NSW in 2019. Cecile was one of the organising co-chairs of ACL-COLING 2006 in Sydney, as well as local sponsorship chair of ACL 2018.

Gholamreza Haffari, Professor and ARC Future Fellow at the Department of Data Science & AI, Monash University, Melbourne, Australia, Director of Vision and Language (AI) Research.
email: Gholamreza.Haffari@monash.edu
website: https://users.monash.edu.au/~gholamrh/
Prof Gholamreza (Reza) Haffari has published numerous papers in the top-tier NLP venues, including the main ACL conference and served as senior area-chair and reviewer of these conferences as well. He teaches different courses in Monash university, including NLP and Machine learning subjects. Reza has co-presented a tutorial at HLT-NAAC 2006 (Inductive Semi-supervised Learning Methods: with Applicability to Natural Language Processing), and a tutorial at Machine Translation Summit XII 2009 (Machine Learning Approaches for Dealing with Limited Bilingual Data in Statistical Machine Translation). He has mentored 70+ postdoctoral fellows and PhD/MSc students throughout his career. This has provided him with an extensive experience about the needs of early career researchers for effective communication of their research.

Vulnerabilities of Large Language Models to Adversarial Attacks

Yu Fu, Erfan Shayegan, Md. Mamun Al Abdullah, Pedram Zaree, Nael Abu-Ghazaleh and Yue Dong

This tutorial serves as a comprehensive guide on the vulnerabilities of Large Language Models (LLMs) to adversarial attacks, an interdisciplinary field that blends perspectives from Natural Language Processing (NLP) and Cybersecurity. As LLMs become more complex and integrated into various systems, understanding their security attributes is crucial. However, current research indicates that even safety-aligned models are not impervious to adversarial attacks that can result in incorrect or harmful outputs. The tutorial first lays the foundation by explaining safety-aligned LLMs and concepts in cybersecurity. It then categorizes existing research based on different types of learning architectures and attack methods. We highlight the existing vulnerabilities of unimodal LLMs, multi-modal LLMs, and systems that integrate LLMs, focusing on adversarial attacks designed to exploit weaknesses and mislead AI systems. Finally, the tutorial delves into the potential causes of these vulnerabilities and discusses potential defense mechanisms.

Yu Fu, Ph.D. candidate in Computer Science and Engineering at UC Riverside.
email: `yfu093@ucr.edu`
website: `https://fyyfu.github.io/`
He is a first-year Ph.D student advised by Prof. Yue Dong. His research interests lie in natural language processing and machine learning. His recent research focuses on safety alignments, watermarking text generation models, and reducing hallucinations in large language models.

Erfan Shayegani, Ph.D. Candidate in Computer Science and Engineering at UC Riverside.
email: `sshay004@ucr.edu`
website: `https://erfanshayegani.github.io/`
He is a Ph.D student advised by Prof. Yue Dong and Prof. Nael AbuGhazaleh. His research interests lie at the intersection of Generative AI and Systems, with topics spanning NLP, Alignment, and Scalability/Security/Privacy within the domain of Large (Vision) Language Models (LLMs), Multi-Modal Foundation Models, and Text-3D models such as NeRF. His keen interest lies in integrating these complex models into sophisticated systems, where he takes an adversarial approach to uncover vulnerabilities and strengthen their trustworthiness, safety, and scalability. He holds a B.Sc. in Electrical Engineering from Sharif University of Technology.

Proceedings of the 62nd Annual Meeting of the Association for Computational Linguistics (Volume 5: Tutorial Abstracts), pages 8–9
August 11-16, 2024 ©2024 Association for Computational Linguistics

Md. Mamun Al Abdullah, Ph.D. Candidate in Computer Science and Engineering at UC Riverside.
email: mmamu003@ucr.edu
website: https://sites.google.com/view/aamamun
He is a Ph.D. student advised by Prof. Nael Abu-Ghazaleh. His research focuses on system security.

Pedram Zaree, Ph.D. Candidate in Computer Science and Engineering at UC Riverside.
email: pzare003@ucr.edu
website: https://pedramzaree.github.io/
He is a Ph.D. student in Computer Science and Engineering at UC Riverside, advised by Prof. Nael Abu-Ghazaleh. His research focuses on the security of retrieval-based NLP systems, security of machine learning systems, and AR/VR systems. He also has a background in electrical engineering since he has completed a B.Sc program in the Electrical Engineering department at Sharif University of Technology.

Nael Abu-Ghazaleh, Professor in the Computer Science and Engineering Department at the University of California, Riverside.
email: naelag@ucr.edu
website: https://www.cs.ucr.edu/ nael/
His research is in computer systems, with emphasis on security of emerging systems. His group has developed a number of new attacks on CPUs, GPUs, AR/VR devices and operating systems, that have been reported to industry and resulted in patches and changes to consumer products. He is currently serving as the co-general chair of ASPLOS'24 and PACT'24, and as the program chair of SEED'24. He is an ACM Distinguished Member, an IEEE Distinguished lecturer, and a member of the IEEE Micro Hall of Fame.

Yue Dong, Assistant Professor in Computer Science and Engineering at the University of California, Riverside.
email: yued@ucr.edu
website: https://yuedong.us/
She leads the Natural Language Processing group, which develops NLP systems that are trustworthy, safe and efficient. She served as senior area chair for AACL'23 and area chair for EMNLP'22 & '23, and has co-organized workshops at EMNLP'21 & '23, NeurIPS'21 & 22 &'23, and tutorials at NAACL'22 and KDD'23.

Watermarking for Large Language Model

Xuandong Zhao, Yu-Xiang Wang and Lei Li

As AI-generated text increasingly resembles human-written content, the ability to detect machine-generated text becomes crucial in both the computational linguistics and machine learning communities. In this tutorial, we aim to provide an in-depth exploration of text watermarking, a subfield of linguistic steganography with the goal of embedding a hidden message (the watermark) within a text passage. We will introduce the fundamentals of text watermarking, discuss the main challenges in identifying AI-generated text, and delve into the current watermarking methods, assessing their strengths and weaknesses. Moreover, we will explore other possible applications of text watermarking and discuss future directions for this field. Each section will be supplemented with examples and key takeaways.

Xuandong Zhao, Ph.D. Candidate in Computer Science at the University of California, Santa Barbara.
email: `xuandongzhao@cs.ucsb.edu`
website: `https://xuandongzhao.github.io`
He is advised by Professors Yu-Xiang Wang and Lei Li. His research combines machine learning and natural language processing to build ethical and trustworthy generative AI systems. He has published several papers in leading NLP/ML conferences such as ACL, NAACL, EMNLP, ICML, AISTATS, and UAI. In addition to his research, Xuandong has actively participated in the academic community, serving on the Program Committee for ACL/EMNLP 2022/2023, ICML 2023, NeurIPS 2023, and ICLR 2024. His professional experience extends beyond academia, having completed internships at industry giants including Microsoft, Google, and Alibaba. Xuandong is the recipient of the prestigious Chancellor's Fellowship from UC Santa Barbara. He obtained his Bachelor of Science degree in Computer Science from Zhejiang University in 2019.

Yu-Xiang Wang, Faculty Member of the Computer Science Department at UCSB.
email: `yuxiangw@cs.ucsb.edu`
website: `https://sites.cs.ucsb.edu/yuxiangw`
Prior to joining UCSB, he was a scientist with Amazon AI in Palo Alto. Even before that he was with the Machine Learning Department at Carnegie Mellon University and had the pleasure of being jointly advised by Stephen Fienberg, Alex Smola, Ryan Tibshirani and Jing Lei. Over the years Yu-Xiang has worked on a diverse set of problems in the broad area of statistical machine learning, e.g., trend filtering, differential privacy, subspace clustering, large-scale learning / optimization, bandits / reinforcement learning, just to name a few. His

Proceedings of the 62nd Annual Meeting of the Association for Computational Linguistics (Volume 5: Tutorial Abstracts), pages 10–11
August 11-16, 2024 ©2024 Association for Computational Linguistics

most recent quests include making differential privacy practical and developing a statistical foundation for off-policy reinforcement learning.

Lei Li, Assistant Professor in the Language Technology Institute at Carnegie Mellon University
email: `leili@cs.cmu.edu`
website: `https://lileicc.github.io`
His research interest lies in natural language processing, machine translation, and AI-powered drug discovery. He received his B.S. from Shanghai Jiao Tong University and Ph.D. from Carnegie Mellon University. His dissertation work on fast algorithms for mining co-evolving time series was awarded ACM KDD best dissertation (runner up). His recent work on AI writer Xiaomingbot received 2nd-class award of Wu Wen-tsün AI prize in 2017. He is a recipient of ACL 2021 best paper award, CCF Young Elite award in 2019, and CCF distinguished speaker in 2017. His team won first places for five language translation directions in WMT 2020 and the best in corpus filtering challenge. Previously, he worked at ByteDance as the founding director of AI Lab. He has served organizers and area chair/senior PC for multiple conferences including KDD, ACL, EMNLP, ICML, ICLR, NeurIPS, AAAI, IJCAI, and CIKM. He has started ByteDance's machine translation system, VolcTrans and many of his algorithms have been deployed in production.